Heathcliff's creator, George Gately, has been plagued by "cartoonitis" since he was a child. In grammar school, his fourth grade art teacher gave the class an assignment to draw a picture depicting something from the American Revolution. George titled his picture "George Washington Crossing the Delaware," drew an empty body of water with a few bubbles surfacing and subtitled it "The Boat Sank." George didn't get a very good mark in Art that month.

He did better later on when he started freelance cartooning. His first major sale was to the *Saturday Evening Post*. Since then he has appeared in just about every leading magazine in the United States, Canada, Europe, South America and around the world. His work has even been displayed at a cartoon exhibit in the Louvre in Paris!

Thank goodness a cure for "cartoonitis" has never been discovered.

HEATHCLIFF

by George Gately

tempo
books

GROSSET & DUNLAP
PUBLISHERS · NEW YORK
A Filmways Company

"OH, OH!"

"STOP KIDDING! I KNOW HEATHCLIFF'S A TOUGH CAT, BUT DON'T TELL ME HE'S SCARING THE ELEPHANTS!"

"EMMA!...DID YOU HEAR THAT?!...I NEVER HEARD PRETTY BOY HIT SUCH A HIGH NOTE!"

"HEATHCLIFF PACKED HIS OWN LUNCH."

"HEATHCLIFF! CUT THAT OUT!!"

"STICK 'EM UP!"

"STRAIGHT DOWN THE ROAD... AS THE CROW FLIES."

"HE'S OVER HERE, GRAMPS...MAKING FACES AT A SHARK."

"SHE LOVES ME... SHE LOVES ME NOT..."

"NOW I'LL *NEVER* KNOW!"

"NEVER FEAR, SIR... HE CAN BE TAUGHT TO OBEY."

"WATCH OUT FOR MUGGSY FABER!...HE'S GOING
TO TIE A FIRECRACKER TO HEATHCLIFF'S TAIL!"

"WIPED OUT!"

"WE CAUGHT THREE BASS, AND HEATHCLIFF
CAUGHT AN ELECTRIC EEL."

"HE DOESN'T LIKE LASSIE."

"HE COMES HERE QUITE OFTEN."

"I WAS ADMIRING THE BABY AND IT HISSED AT ME!"

"THAT'S A FINE WAY TO BRING ME MY NEWSPAPER!"

"HEATHCLIFF BETTER BEWARE OF OL' SARGE!
... SARGE IS A POLICE DOG!"

"IT'S FOR YOU."

"MY GOSH!...THIS IS THE EIGHTH TIME YOU'VE HAD THIS CLOCK IN FOR REPAIRS, MRS. NUTMEG!"

"CUCKOO!"

"MRS. NUTMEG, WILL HEATHCLIFF EAT LEFTOVERS?"

"SUNNY AND MILD TODAY..."

"... AND TONIGHT..."

"HE'S PRACTICING HIS PUTTING."

"HE'S ORGANIZED A SING-A-LONG!"

"NO PETS ALLOWED IN MY CAB, LADY!"

"THEY'RE DINING BY CANDLELIGHT."

"HEATHCLIFF COLLECTS THEM."

"GRANDMA, DID YOU KNOW CATS WERE WORSHIPED
IN ANCIENT EGYPT?"

"OH, OH!... I FORGOT THE CAT FOOD!"

"HEATHCLIFF!"

"I THINK I CAN HANDLE IT, THANK YOU!"

"I THINK I FIGURED OUT A WAY TO STOP HEATHCLIFF FROM WRECKING THAT CUCKOO CLOCK."

"THAT'S HIM ON THE LEFT, OFFICER...
HE MUGGED MY HAT!"

"HE DOESN'T LIKE YOUR ACT."

" HEATHCLIFF, IT'S FOR Y- "

"SOMEBODY PINNED THE TAIL ON HEATHCLIFF!"

"YOU GOTTA ADMIT HE'S AWFULLY GOOD!"

"GET HIM OUT OF HERE!"

"HE DOESN'T LIKE YOUR COAT!"

"OH MY, OH MY!
HOW CUTE! HOW CUTE!...

... LET ME SEE BABY!
COOCHY, COOCHY, COO!"

"HE'S BEEN BUSTED FOR FELINE DELINQUENCY!"

"...AND COMING OUT OF CHUTE NUMBER TWO...."

"WHAT'S HE DONE NOW?!"

Dear Kitty Mush Co.,
I am writing in behalf of a friend about your crummy cat food....
© 1974 McNaught Synd., Inc

"THAT'S HIS MATING CALL."

"THE GRIEVANCE COMMITTEE IS HERE TO SEE YOU."

"NO, WE HAVE ONLY ONE CAT, BUT HE'S A BIT SPOILED."

"NEXT."

"D-DID YOU HEAR SOMETHING PURR?!"

"NEXT, WE MUST VOTE ON A REQUEST FOR A
MUNICIPAL SCRATCHING POST."

"GOT ANYTHING FOR A PARROT?"

"LOOK, DEAR!...KITTY JUST LOVES NEW AND
IMPROVED 'MEW-MEW LIVER LUMPS'!"

"GRAMPS!...HEATHCLIFF IS USING THE
TRAMPOLINE AGAIN!"

12-11

DANGER
THIN
ICE

"I'D SWEAR THAT LITTLE BABY SWIPED A HERRING!"

"HEATHCLIFF SEEMED TO ENJOY MOUNT RUSHMORE."

"A MOUSE IN YOUR KITCHEN, MRS. CLANCY ?!...
HEATHCLIFF WILL BE RIGHT OVER !"

"HE MAKES HOUSE CALLS ?!"

"POUR YOUR OWN!"

" WHAT'S NEW, PUSSYCAT ? "

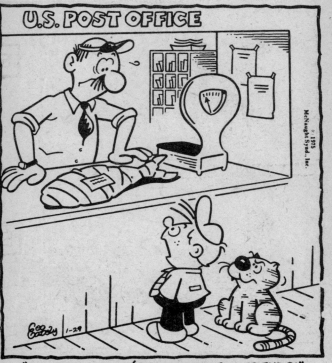

"YOU MEAN HE CAN'T MAIL A GIFT TO A FRIEND?!"

"THERE!... HE'S COMFY... IS EVERYONE SATISFIED?!"

"AFTER ALL...IT'S NOT WHETHER YOU WIN OR LOSE,
BUT HOW YOU PLAY THE GAME!"

"IT'S THAT SMART-ALEC CAT AGAIN!"

"HE KNOCKS OVER EVERY CAN IN THE NEIGHBORHOOD...

... AND THEN HE USES A FINGER BOWL!"

"SOUNDS LIKE HEATHCLIFF WHEN SOMEBODY STEPS ON HIS TAIL."

"WHO'S THE ONE IN THE TOUPEE?!"

"NO HANDOUTS!"

"WHO PASTED THAT BUMPER STICKER ON THERE?!"

GRRRRRRR

© 1974
McNaught Synd., Inc.

9-10

"ON THAT FISH MARKET BREAK-IN...SUSPECT IN CUSTODY."

"I'LL DO THE DUCK CALLS!"

"YOU TEAR OUT THE CAT FOOD COUPONS *AFTER* I'VE READ THE PAPER!"

© 1975
McNaught Synd., Inc. 1-22

"THEY'RE IN THE BACKYARD PLAYING COWBOYS AND INDIANS."

"AND NOW BACK TO OUR MOVIE ...
'CURSE OF THE CAT PEOPLE'..."

"I NEVER THOUGHT I'D BE EXPELLED AT MY AGE!"

"GRANDMA, HEATHCLIFF DOESN'T LIKE YOU TO
SHOW HIS BABY PICTURES!"

"I THOUGHT *YOU* LOCKED HIM IN THE HOUSE!!"

"IF YOU SAY ANYTHING TO THIS GUY,
SAY SOMETHING NICE!"

"HAVE YOU SEEN MY DOG, ROLLO?...HE'S A BOXER."

"HAS ANYONE SEEN THE BOOK I WAS READING?"

"THAT'S NOT IT!"

"I THINK HE'S BREAKING IN A NITE CLUB ACT."

"I'LL SEE IF THE SULTAN IS IN."

"I BROUGHT CHAMP OVER TO APOLOGIZE
FOR PICKING ON HEATHCLIFF."

"WE DON'T NEED THE MICE, THANK YOU."

"HEATHCLIFF WANTS TO GO TO WORK WITH YOU...
HE HEARD YOU MENTION THE RAT RACE."

"SOMETIMES I THINK HE'S IN CONSUMER RESEARCH!"

"WHO'S BEEN PLAYING WITH MY HAIRSPRAY?!"

"NOW TO GET BACK TO MY STILL LIFE."

"LOOKS LIKE YOUR DOG'S BEEN DIAPERED."

"YOU'D BETTER LAY OFF THAT UMPIRE!"

"THERE GOES THE MILKMAN, RATTLING BOTTLES AGAIN!!"

"SHUCKS, HEATHCLIFF...
THERE'S NOTHIN' TO DO!"

"NO...I DON'T WANT TO DUMP GARBAGE CANS."

© 1975 McNaught Synd., Inc.

"ANY MORE HISSING FROM THIS DUGOUT AND
I'M SENDING YOU TO THE SHOWERS!"

" SAY, WHAT KIND OF A BUG IS ...

...WAS THAT ? "